The Cowgirl's Cookbook

The Cowgirl's Cookbook

*Recipes for Your Home
on the Range*

Jill Charlotte Stanford

TWODOT®

GUILFORD, CONNECTICUT
HELENA, MONTANA
AN IMPRINT OF THE GLOBE PEQUOT PRESS

A · T W O D O T® · B O O K

Text design by Nancy Freeborn

Library of Congress Cataloging-in-Publication Data is available on file.

ISBN 978-0-7627-4512-8

Printed in Korea

15 14 13 12

I dedicate this to all the real Cowboy Girls.
Especially to Joan and Joanna, my trail pals.

And to my sister, Robin Johnson, who never lets me quit
and who keeps the herd from stampeding.

Contents

Acknowledgments

It is impossible to write and compile a book without a little help—just as you can't move a herd without outriders.

My thanks go first of all to Anne Bothner-By, my longtime friend and computer guru who put it all together for Globe Pequot Press.

My sister, Robin Johnson, helped me with the recipes, contributing some and testing quite a few. Her culinary expertise was welcome.

Rebecca Lintz, director of the Colorado Historic Society was heroic in her efforts to get images to me.

Coi Gehrit at the Denver Public Library was interested in the project; she made some wonderful suggestions and was terrifically helpful.

Polly Helm, the Pendleton Cowgirl Company trail boss, made sure I got what I asked for, even though she is in the Peace Corps and far, far away. Gracias, mi amigo.

Anthony DiGreggorio of New World Records was diligent in his efforts to trace the copyright to "I Want To Be a Real Cowboy Girl."

Dear Cousin Tommy Rentschler, who told me about "cackleberries," wrote to me, "Cowgirls Rule," and has obtained Honorary Cowboy status.

My editors, Megan Hiller, Erin Turner, Gia Manalio, and Amy Paradysz. All of them put their brand on the manuscript as it went down the trail.

To all the cowgirls who shared with me their stories, photos, recipes, and encouragement, I tip my hat. Trophy buckles all around!

I Want To Be a Real Cowboy Girl

I love all the roar and the rattle,
the lure and the bellow of cattle,
and I love to see the cowboys
at the ro-de-o.

The quirt I can hear it stingin,'
and I can see the lariats swingin,'
and my heart is always happy
at the ro-de-o.

(chorus)
I want to be a real cowboy girl
and wear all the buckles and straps
and know how it feels to wear spurs on your heels
then strut around in my chaps.

I want to tote a six-shooter too.
wear a belt that is four inches wide
then ride like the deuce on a buckskin cayuse
with a cowboy I love at my side.

I dream of a song and it lingers
in my heart I can hear all the singers
As they sing of love and friendship
at the ro-de-o.

How I'd love to ride in the open
on a great big cayuse just a lopin'
I'd be happy with my cowboy
at the ro-de-o.

(chorus)
I want to be a real cowboy girl
and wear all the buckles and straps
and know how it feels to have spurs on my heels
then strut about in my chaps.

I want to wear a ten-gallon hat,
wear a belt that is four inches wide,
and bulldog a steer at the fair every year
and jump on my pony and ride!

—C. PRENTIS FORRESTER

Sung originally by the Girls of the Golden
West in 1935 on a Victor-Bluebird label
and included in an anthology of American
Cowboy Songs "Back in the Saddle Again,"
released by New World Records in 1983.

Preface

My lifelong ambition has been to be a cowgirl.

Cowgirls rode and roped with the best of the cowboys on the silver screen. Mounted on flashy steeds, wearing western-style clothing complete with fringe and silver belt buckles, cowgirls seemed to me to have it all.

Without a hair out of place and their makeup perfectly applied, I saw that there could be no better life in the world than loping across the prairies and occasionally joining in song around the campfire at night with the buckaroos.

It goes without saying that Dale Evans was my role model.

Cowgirls were always cheerful and resourceful and were never in the kitchen, and there never seemed to be any children to slow them down.

It seemed to be a free and glamorous life, and that's the life I wanted, too.

Not very many years ago, I found a picture of some early-day cowgirls, taken about 1915. What a bunch! Everyone in the photo is grinning and the clothes speak of individualism in the truest western-style.

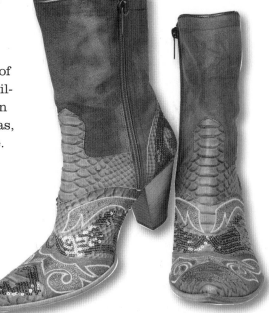

When I grew up and met some real cowgirls, a few of my illusions were shattered. Quite often there were children. And there were the duties of a wife to attend to in the kitchen, no matter how small or inconvenient it was, or even out on those dreamed-of prairies by a campfire.

This was a sobering fact.

On the other hand, the basic style of the cowgirl as I imagined her to be was—and still is—intact.

Cowgirls really are cheerful and resourceful. They nearly always look the part in western-style clothes— even when they are faded blue jeans and scuffed boots. They don't always ride flashy horses, but they can often out-ride and out-rope their counterparts, the cowboys.

Cowgirls have always been, and still are, straight shooters. They are loyal and brave and imaginative. They can make a meal at a gallop and make it look easy.

I want you to meet a few of my heroines. I hope you will sample their cooking and get a taste of their lives.

And when I finally go to the Big Prairie in the Sky, I hope St. Peter will greet me and smile and say, "Ride on, Cowgirl!"

—JILL CHARLOTTE STANFORD, 2008

"When a cowgirl dies and goes to Heaven, she does not get a halo. Instead, she gets a big, silver belt buckle."

—JILL CHARLOTTE STANFORD

Beverages

BEA KIRNAN   PRAIRIE ROSE   MABLE STRICKLAND   PRINCIS MOHAWK   RUTH ROACH   KITTIE CANUTT   PRAIRIE LILLIE

Prairie Rose's Desert Rose

1 jigger (4 ounces) tequila
1–2 drops Tabasco sauce
Shaker of salt
Wedge of lime

Prairie Rose Henderson was one of the early cowgirls who wore flamboyant outfits and competed in rodeos right alongside the cowboys. She was a great crowd-pleaser. When not competing, she rode trick horses. She might have enjoyed this pick-me-up to soothe her aching muscles following a performance. Or, perhaps, before a show. She died in 1937 in a snowstorm.

Pour tequila into a small clear highball glass. Gently add Tabasco to the tequila. Watch as it forms a rose shape in the glass. Lick the V between your thumb and index finger. Sprinkle with salt. Take a bite of lime, lick the salt, and down the hatch with the "rose." Chase with another bite of lime.

Serves 1

Sangria

2 oranges, cut in wedges
1 lemon, cut in wedges
1 lime, cut in wedges
1 cup strawberries or raspberries (you can use frozen, then thawed)
1 8-ounce can (4 slices) of pineapple slices
1/2 cup sugar
Fifth of Burgundy wine
8–10 oz. club soda
Ice

Cut the fruit and squeeze the fruit quarters to extract the juice into a tall glass pitcher. Then put in the rinds and sugar. Add the pineapple slices, also cut into fourths. Stir with a wooden spoon until everything is all "muddled up."

Add the wine, then slowly add the soda. Stir well.

Pour into tall, ice-filled glasses and garnish with orange slices.

Serves 6

After a long day's ride on the trails, what better way to watch the sun go down than with a pitcher of this flavorful and potent drink and several equally trail-weary but happy friends.

*"Horses . . .
Proof that God loves us and
wants us to be happy."*

—SEEN ON A T-SHIRT

It can get awfully hot and dusty in the corrals during branding and roundup time. This thirst-quencher was served in tin cups during a lunch break at a roundup outside of Ontario, Oregon. I was lucky enough to be asked to help and trailered my horse, Tune, and myself four hundred miles just to be a part of a vanishing way of life.

I am still not certain just how much help I was—Tune was no help at all—but the cowboys were patient and kind and saw to it that I didn't get into too much trouble.

Cow Punchers Punch

4 cups very strong brewed and chilled iced tea, made
4 cups chilled apple juice
2 cups unsweetened pineapple juice
2 1-liter (or 33.8 fl. oz.) bottles club soda
Lemon slices

Combine all ingredients and stir well.

Serves 10–12 thirsty hands

Watermelon Ice

2 cups diced, seeded watermelon
1 cup light corn syrup
2 tablespoons lime juice

In a large bowl, mash the watermelon until smooth. Add the corn syrup and lime juice. Stir well. Cover and freeze two to three hours until almost firm. Beat with a wooden spoon until firm, then freeze again.

Spoon into short 8 oz. glasses and provide spoons.

You can add 1 jigger of tequila per serving for an extra "kick."

Makes about 4 cups

Breads

A great favorite, both around the campfire or while cozied up in front of a fire, is old-fashioned cornbread. Served with chili or soup, this one—courtesy of Janet Larson, a cowgirl who is at home on the range as well as in front of one in her kitchen near Mitchell, Oregon—is fast and easy and has a few surprises that make it pretty darned special.

Just like Cowgirls.

A Cowgirl's Cornbread

1½ cups yellow cornmeal
1 cup whole wheat flour
1 cup unbleached white flour
1 tablespoon baking powder
1 teaspoon baking soda
1 teaspoon salt
2 cups buttermilk or plain yogurt
½ cup milk
¼ cup maple syrup, brown sugar, or honey
2 eggs, beaten
¼ cup butter, melted and cooled

Preheat oven to 350 degrees. Butter a 9x13-inch baking pan or a 2-inch-deep round iron skillet.

Sift the dry ingredients into a large bowl.

In another bowl, combine all the wet ingredients and stir until mixed. Fold the wet ingredients into the dry ingredients. Smooth the batter into the pan or skillet and bake for 25–30 minutes or until a straw inserted in the center comes out clean.

Cool for at least 10 minutes before cutting.

Makes 12 pieces

"There are 2 theories to arguing with a woman . . . neither works."

—WILL ROGERS

Buttermilk Honey Biscuits

2 cups flour
2 teaspoons baking powder
1/2 teaspoon baking soda
1 teaspoon salt
1/4 cup shortening
1 cup buttermilk (powdered will do fine)
1/4 cup honey

Sift the dry ingredients into a large bowl. Cut the shortening in with a fork until it resembles cornmeal. Add the buttermilk and honey and mix well.

Roll out the dough to a thickness of 1 inch and then cut out rounds using a glass. Place in a lightly greased pan and bake at 350 degrees until golden brown.

Serve with Oregon Grape Jelly (page 84)

Makes 16 biscuits

"Don't screw with me, fellas.
This ain't my first time
at the rodeo."
—LULU PARR

Lulu Bell Parr

(1876–1955) was an independent and spirited Wild West performer who thrilled audiences across the world with her daring feats. She rode in some of the most famous Wild West shows of the last century. Once she rode horseback for approximately 600 miles from Pennsylvania to Ohio to visit relatives. When asked why such a long trip on horseback, she simply said she and her horse were tired of the steam trains.

Annie Oatley Bread

1 package regular dry yeast (not rapid rise)

1/2 cup packed brown sugar, divided

2 cups boiling water, divided

1 cup old-fashioned oatmeal

1 teaspoon salt

1/2 tablespoon butter

4 cups bread flour

Put yeast and 1 teaspoon of brown sugar in a small bowl. Pour 1/4 cup of boiling water on the yeast and sugar and stir until combined. Set aside.

In a large bowl, combine the oatmeal, salt, and butter and then pour the remaining boiling water over the mixture. Stir well until the butter is melted. Cool this mixture over a bowl of cold water until lukewarm (about 100 degrees).

Add the yeast mixture and flour to the oatmeal mixture and stir until well combined. Cover the bowl with plastic wrap and place in the refrigerator to rise overnight.

In the morning, unwrap the dough and stir again. Cover with plastic wrap and let rise again on the counter away from any drafts, about 1 1/2 hours, or until double in size.

Oil a loaf pan. Punch or stir the dough down, let it rest a few minutes, and then put it into the loaf pan. Use lightly wet fingers to shape it into a loaf. Let the dough rise again about 1 hour, covered with a lightly oiled piece of plastic wrap.

Preheat oven to 350 degrees. Bake the loaf for about 40 minutes. The old-fashioned method of testing for doneness is to tap the top. It should sound hollow.

Cool on a wire rack before turning out of the pan.

"Any woman who does not thoroughly enjoy tramping across the country on a clear, frosty morning with a good gun and a pair of dogs does not know how to enjoy life."

—ANNIE OAKLEY, 1901

Chuckwagon Doughnuts

2¹/₂ cups all-purpose flour

2 teaspoons salt

1 tablespoon baking soda

2 cups cooking oil, divided

1 cup buttermilk (powdered is okay)

2 brown paper bags—1 filled with 1 cup sugar and
    4 tablespoons cinnamon

In a large bowl, mix the flour, salt, and soda. Add ¹/₃ cup cooking oil and cut it into the flour mixture with a fork. When it resembles cornmeal, shape the dough into an oval, then with your fist make a "well" in the middle. Pour in the buttermilk and stir until it all comes together. Use your hands if you have to.

Flour a flat surface (inside a Dutch oven lid or on a clean, flat rock) and knead the dough 10 or 15 strokes.

Heat the remaining oil in a large iron skillet.

Pinch off balls of dough, flatten them between your palms, and drop into the hot fat.

Fry 2–3 minutes on each side or until golden brown. Drain on one of the brown paper bags and then drop the doughnuts into the other paper bag filled with the sugar-cinnamon mixture. Shake the bag to thoroughly coat the doughnuts.

Makes about 30 doughnuts

*"A cowgirl gets up early in the morning,
decides what she wants to do,
and does it."*

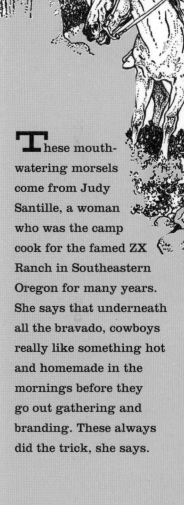

These mouth-watering morsels come from Judy Santille, a woman who was the camp cook for the famed ZX Ranch in Southeastern Oregon for many years. She says that underneath all the bravado, cowboys really like something hot and homemade in the mornings before they go out gathering and branding. These always did the trick, she says.

Cinnamon-Sugar Muffins

1^1/$_2$ cups all-purpose flour
^{3}/$_4$ cup sugar
2 teaspoons baking powder
^{1}/$_4$ teaspoon salt
^{1}/$_4$ teaspoon nutmeg
^{1}/$_2$ cup milk
1 egg, well beaten
^{1}/$_3$ cup, plus 2 tablespoons butter, melted
^{1}/$_2$ cup sugar mixed with 1 teaspoon cinnamon

Preheat oven to 400 degrees. In a medium bowl, mix flour, sugar, baking powder, salt, and nutmeg with a wire whisk. Combine milk, egg, and ^{1}/$_3$ cup melted butter in a small bowl. Pour wet ingredients into dry ingredients and mix well.

Grease muffin tins or use paper liners and fill about two-thirds full. Bake 20 minutes. Brush remaining melted butter over the tops, then sprinkle on the sugar-cinnamon mix.

Makes 12 muffins

Saddlebag Crackers

When the afternoon is lowering toward sunset, Ruth Parmenter likes to saddle up one of the young horses she's training to be a first-class trail horse and ride out onto the buttes by her ranch in eastern Oregon. "We mosey along for a while," she says, pushing her battered straw hat back on her forehead. "Then I'll stop for a little something to eat. I always take along an apple or two—one for me and one for the horse." She is quiet for a moment and then adds, "But only if he's been good and hasn't spooked at anything."

2 cups all-purpose flour, sifted
1 cup yellow cornmeal
1 1/2 teaspoons baking powder
1 1/2 teaspoons salt
3/4 cup shortening
2/3 cup water
2 tablespoons butter, melted

Preheat oven to 425 degrees. Sift the flour, cornmeal, baking powder, and salt together in a large bowl. Work in the shortening until it's coarse. Add the water, a little at a time, and stir lightly until the mixture is damp. Add enough water to hold the dough all together.

Roll out the dough on a lightly floured board to about 1/8-inch thick. Cut into strips, circles, or squares.

Brush the tops with melted butter and, with the tines of a fork, prick each cracker to prevent it from bubbling while baking.

Bake crackers on an ungreased cookie sheet for 10–12 minutes until light brown.

Store in an airtight container.

Makes about 6 dozen crackers

fish &
chicken

Metolius River Salmon Loaf

One of the great mysteries of a cowgirl's pantry is why there is always—and I mean always—a can of tinned salmon in it. If you scrounge around enough, you might also find a box of saltine crackers. Add a few other things found in every cowgirl's pantry, and you are on your way to a delicious casserole, like the one I was served as luncheon fare by a woman who was retired from the rigors of ranch life and told me hair-raising tales of pulling calves in snowstorms and loose cinches. The background music to this pleasant afternoon was the sound of the Metolius River rushing by her cabin.

1 egg
1/4 cup undiluted evaporated milk
1 cup crumbled saltine crackers or soft bread crumbs
1 tablespoon butter, melted
Salt and pepper to taste
2 cups tinned salmon, drained and flaked

Preheat the oven to 400 degrees. Beat together egg, milk, crumbled crackers or bread crumbs, melted butter, salt, and pepper.

Mix the salmon and crumb mixture together and pour into a greased loaf pan. Bake for 30 minutes or until set. Serve hot with tomato sauce or sliced cold with mayonnaise.

Serves 6

"A good cook can catch a feller."

—MARY KETTLE, 1905, Eastern Washington Homesteader

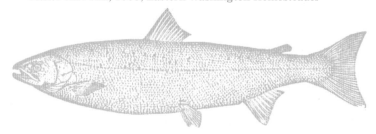

Streamside Brook Trout

2 fresh trout
4 tablespoons bacon fat wrapped in aluminum foil or plastic wrap
2 tablespoons flour in a plastic bag
Iron skillet

"Clean the trout, leaving on the tails, but cut off the heads. They take up too much room in the skillet. Get the fire going hot, put the skillet over the coals, and melt the bacon fat. Dredge the trout in the flour right in the bag, then lay them in the sizzling fat. Brown one side, about 3 minutes. Pick them up by the tail and turn them over to brown the other side. Use the bag for the bones and take them with you when you leave. Make sure your fire is out by dousing it with water, then kicking dirt over the wet coals. Use the gravel from the stream or lake to clean your frying pan."

Serves 2, or 1 hungry cowgirl/fisherperson

Rivers, lakes, and streams abound out in the West. Trout lurk about in the cold waters, and you might see Sally Hutchins lurking about on the bank with a rod and reel in her hands. Tied to a tree or shrub nearby is her horse and only companion on these fishing trips, Buster.

In his saddlebags, Buster carries a cast-iron skillet, a tin plate and fork, some flour in a large zipped-tight plastic bag, and a little bacon fat in a discarded "snoose" can. He waits patiently for Sally to catch her limit—two. Then she builds a little fire; cleans and cooks her catch; tosses it about in the flour in the bag; heats the bacon fat in the skillet until it's smoking; fries the fish; eats it; washes the pan, plate, and fork; puts the fire out—twice for good measure; repacks the saddlebags; mounts Buster; and rides home to her little cabin. It has been a perfect day for Sally. Buster, too.

The Bunk House Favorite Tuna-Egg Casserole

2 tablespoons butter

1 cup chopped celery

1 can cream of mushroom soup

1/2 cup water

1 can tuna, drained

2 teaspoons grated lemon peel (but only if you have it)

4 hard-cooked eggs, sliced

1/2 cup shredded cheese

Preheat oven to 350 degrees.

Melt the butter in a small skillet. Sauté the celery in the butter until almost tender.

In a small bowl combine the mushroom soup and water. Then add the tuna and lemon peel. Add three of the eggs; save one for the top.

Pour mixture into a one-quart casserole dish and bake for 30 minutes. Garnish the top with the shredded cheese and the last egg slices.

Serves 4

Autumn Ride Chicken

4 (8-ounce) boneless, skinless chicken breasts
1 tablespoon butter
2 tablespoons olive oil
1 large shallot, peeled and chopped
3 tablespoons minced fresh tarragon
Salt and pepper to taste
$1/4$ cup dry white wine
Sprigs of fresh tarragon for garnish

Lay each chicken breast between two sheets of plastic wrap and pound firmly with the smooth side of a meat tenderizer or rolling pin. The breasts will almost double in size.

Melt the butter and olive oil in a large skillet and sauté the chopped shallot until golden. Add the chicken, tarragon, salt, and pepper and sauté the chicken breasts over medium heat for 3 minutes on one side. Turn the breasts over, add the wine, and continue cooking for another 3 minutes. Arrange the breasts on a warm plate, spoon the pan juices over the top, and garnish with fresh tarragon.

Serves 4

This chicken dish was served with polenta and a fresh fennel salad dressed with a mustard vinaigrette in a beautiful dining room at the Mio Amore Pensione in Trout Lake, Washington, complete with candles, crystal glasses, and white linen napkins. My dining companions were filthy dirty, tired, and happy to be alive after a hair-raising trail ride through the Mount Adams Wilderness.

Three tired horses were in the horse van outside. The chef and host was gracious, to say the least.

Rattlesnake Stew

Rattlesnakes are sometimes referred to as "desert whitefish."

You will need one medium-size snake (1–2 lbs.).

Remove head, tail, and skin (save and dry to make a hat band in true Cowgirl-style) and clean the snake. Cut the snake into small pieces, cover in flour, and fry in bacon grease or lard. Add seasonings like salt and pepper. A few sagebrush leaves will enhance the flavor.

Cover the snake with water and bring to a boil. Turn down the heat and simmer for 1½ hours or until tender (add additional water if necessary).

While the snake is stewing, melt some bacon fat in a medium saucepan and fry some onions, carrots, celery, and garlic on low until the onions are translucent.

Peel and dice some potatoes.

Add the vegetables to the snake pan and cook slowly until the potatoes are done, about another 30 minutes.

Serves 3–4

"When you are looking for something to eat, a rattlesnake can do just fine."

—MARY S. HAWKINS JOURNAL,
Wyoming Territory, 1899

Hens Arms

2 pounds chicken wings
4 tablespoons vegetable oil
1 cup honey
$^{1}/_{2}$ cup catsup
$^{1}/_{2}$ cup cider vinegar
2 tablespoons, or to taste (optional)

Preheat oven to 325 degrees. In a skillet, heat the oil and fry the wings until golden. (Tuck the end part of the wing under the other two parts to "fold them up.") Drain the wings and put them in a Dutch oven or casserole.

Combine honey, catsup, and vinegar (and soy sauce if desired). Pour this over the chicken, cover and bake for 30 minutes.

Makes approximately 18

These wonderfully named morsels are simple, quick, cheap, and good. My thanks to Shirley Dotten of Parkdale, Oregon, for serving them to me and giving me the recipe. Shirley slipped in as a Cowgirl, even though she raises and trains llamas—not horses—for packing in the mountains. Her knowledge of packing, knots, ropes, and gear is breathtaking, which qualifies her in my opinion.

Beer-Baked Chicken

1 good roasting chicken
1 peeled onion
2 cans beer (one for the chicken and one for you)
Salt (preferably sea salt, but fine granular is fine), to taste

Preheat oven to 330 degrees. Quarter the onion and put it into the cavity of the washed chicken. Place the chicken in a roasting dish and pour 1 can of beer over it. Salt the skin. Roast for about 1 hour, or until the chicken legs move freely and the juices are clear.

A 5-pound chicken will serve four people, with a little left over.

"When things do not go right with you, when the circumstances seem to be against you and Fate deals you a blow between the eyes, remember what the cowboys say in the great Northwest. 'Just grit your teeth, get another hold and let 'er buck!'"

—THE MOTTO OF THE PENDLETON ROUNDUP, 1911.
The Queen that year was Laura McKee.

SCENE AT A SAN LOU'S VALLY CATTLE RANCH.

O.T. DAVIS Phone No.236

O.T.DAVIS PHOTO. 1884

Meats

In 1976, a year of drought in the Oregon eastern desert country, the call went out to anyone with a horse and trailer to help move the cows and calves from the BLM (Bureau of Land Management) land. My friend Peggy Taylor and I loaded our horses into a trailer and made the three-hundred-mile trip to Ontario. We immediately entered another world.

It was hot, dusty, noisy with bawling cows, and acrid with smoke from the branding fires. Dehorning, branding, inoculating, and castrating were all being done simultaneously to the bawling calves. A bucket was nearby, and it was rapidly filling with small bloody hunks of what, I couldn't imagine. The next morning at breakfast, I found out what they were.

Real Cowgirls eat balls.

Rocky Mountain Oysters

12 fresh calf testicles, washed and peeled of the outside skin
   to reveal the "oyster"
2 eggs, beaten
1/2 of a 12-ounce can evaporated milk
2 cups Bisquick
Salt and pepper to taste
1 cup vegetable oil

In a medium bowl, beat the eggs and add the milk. In another bowl, mix the Bisquick, salt, and pepper.

Heat the oil to 350 degrees in a deep skillet.

Dip the "oyster" in the egg and milk mixture, then in the Bisquick. Drop into hot oil and fry until golden brown. Drain on paper towels.

Serves 6
These are not very big—so two per person, along with scrambled eggs and hash-browns would be just about right. And in case you are wondering, they taste like chicken gizzards.

Steak and Beans

For the beans:

2 cups dried pinto beans
1 clove garlic, minced
1 medium onion, peeled and chopped
1/2 cup tomato sauce
2 teaspoons Worcestershire sauce
1 tablespoon bacon grease

Cover the beans with water in a large saucepan and soak for 24 hours. Then add the bacon grease to the soaking water. (This will prevent the beans from boiling over.)

Add the remaining ingredients. Cook at least 8–10 hours over low heat, covered, stirring occasionally. Do not salt while cooking.

For the steak:

1 round steak, about 2 pounds
1/4 cup flour
Salt and pepper, to taste
1 cup whole milk
4 tablespoons vegetable oil

Tenderize the meat by crisscrossing it with a sharp knife, then pounding it with the side of a heavy plate or lid. Roll the tenderized meat in half the flour.

Fry the meat in hot oil for 5 minutes per side. Remove from pan, place it on a platter, and keep it warm in the oven.

Sprinkle remaining flour in the drippings, scraping for the browned bits. Pour in the milk and stir until thickened.

Serve the beans on the side.

Serves 4–6.

It was my good fortune to be introduced to a woman who had cooked real ranch fare nearly all of her life. Lila was as tough as some of the steaks she prepared. She shared this recipe with me, assuring me that this was "the real thing" and that men loved it. She said her mother cooked the same thing when she was growing up, but that her mother "didn't have any garlic. I guess I modernized it somewhat."

Emergency Steak

1 pound hamburger
1 tablespoon minced onion
¹/₂ cup milk
Salt and pepper to taste
Dash of Worcestershire sauce
¹/₄ cup bread crumbs
1 6.5-ounce can of mushroom stems
   and pieces

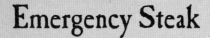

Smush all the ingredients—except the mushrooms—
together with your (washed) wet hands and place on a
lightly greased frying pan. Pat the mixture into the shape
of a T-bone steak, 1-inch thick. Cover with the mushrooms
and broil until rare, medium rare, or well done.

Serves 4

Rocky Mt.
Denv

Cajun Meat Loaf

Seasoning mix:
2 whole bay leaves
1 tablespoon salt
1 teaspoon ground red pepper
1 teaspoon black pepper
1/2 teaspoon white pepper
1/2 teaspoon ground cumin
1/2 teaspoon ground nutmeg

Meat Loaf:
4 tablespoons butter
3/4 cup finely chopped onions
1/2 cup finely chopped celery
1/2 cup finely chopped green peppers
1/4 cup finely chopped green onions
2 teaspoons minced garlic
1 tablespoon Tabasco sauce
1 tablespoon Worcestershire sauce
1/2 cup evaporated milk
1/2 cup ketchup
2 pounds ground elk
2 eggs, slightly beaten
1 cup fine dry bread crumbs

Combine the seasoning mix ingredients in a small bowl and set aside.

Melt butter in a Dutch oven over medium heat. Add onions, celery, peppers, green onions, garlic, Tabasco sauce, Worcestershire sauce, and seasoning mix. Sauté, stirring occasionally, until mixture starts sticking to the bottom of the Dutch oven. Stir in milk and ketchup and continue cooking for about 2 minutes, stirring occasionally.

Remove from heat and allow to cool to room temperature. Remove bay leaves.

Preheat oven to 350 degrees. Add ground elk, eggs, and bread crumbs to cooled vegetable mix. Mix by hand until thoroughly combined. Shape into loaf and bake, uncovered, for 25 minutes. Turn up the oven to 400 degrees and bake for an additional 35 minutes. If baking in the ground, bake covered for approximately 1 hour.

Serves 6

You will never want to make any other meat loaf after you have tried this one from Jean Brown, "way up the Salmon River in Idaho." She says, "This is a favorite dish at the cowboy dinners we have in our home." She uses elk meat in this recipe, but you can also use a good lean ground beef.

If you didn't bag an elk this year, you can order it from someone who did. Sisters Harvest Basket P.O. Box 1961 Sisters, Oregon 97759 (541) 549–0598 They have buffalo too!

Mock Filet Mignon— Venison Back

1 (2–3 pound) venison fillet
2 cups buttermilk
Salt and pepper to taste
6 slices bacon

Slice the venison across the grain into six 1½-inch fillets. Place in a pan and cover with buttermilk. Cover and refrigerate overnight.

Remove the venison from the buttermilk and rinse. Dry and season with salt and pepper. Wrap a bacon slice around the edge of one steak, securing with a toothpick. Repeat with the remaining five.

Grill the venison under high heat, 4–6 inches from the broiler, or over a flame for 6–8 minutes for medium, less for rare.

Serves 6

Every Cowboy has a rifle, and every Cowgirl knows what to do with the venison that is brought in. Heck—most Cowgirls have rifles as well. The tenderloin or fillet of deer is the choicest cut. Soaking in buttermilk reduces the wild or gamy taste.

Whiskey Lamb

1/2 cup butter

1/3 cup vegetable oil

1 clove garlic, minced

1/2 cup minced onion

1/2 cup whiskey

1/2 cup orange juice with pulp

1/4 cup maple syrup

4 tablespoons dark molasses

2 tablespoons soy sauce

1 tablespoon freshly grated ginger

Salt and pepper to taste

3 tablespoons cornstarch

3 tablespoons grated orange peel

1 (4–6 pound) leg of lamb, trimmed of excess fat

To prepare the glaze, melt the butter over low heat in a medium saucepan. Add the oil, garlic, and onion and sauté until golden. Turn the heat up to medium hot and add the rest of the ingredients except the cornstarch and orange peel.

Gradually add the cornstarch to the mixture, stirring until it reaches a glaze consistency. Stir in the orange peel.

Generously brush the glaze all over the top and sides of the lamb.

Cook the lamb over a hot barbecue for 40 minutes for medium rare, turning frequently and brushing on additional glaze with each turning.

If using an oven, roast at 350 degrees for 45 minutes for medium rare, brushing on more glaze every 10 minutes or so.

Serves 4–6

I am well aware of the strong feelings between ranchers with cattle and ranchers with sheep. But, throwing caution to the wind, I am sharing with you what I think is a real Cowgirl recipe for leg of lamb that just might change the minds of any rancher with cattle you happen to serve this to.

Of all the ingredients listed, the whiskey ought to be the easiest to find if you are a real Cowgirl. The rest might mean a trip to the store down the road in the pickup truck. The maple syrup, orange juice, and molasses, aside from the lamb and whiskey, are the most important ingredients. The rest are embellishments, like silver conchas on your belt. Feel free to experiment. If no one likes it, just pour yourself a thimble of whiskey and you will feel much better.

Red-Eye Gravy n' Ham

2 tablespoons vegetable oil
4 ham steaks, 1/4-inch thick
1 cup water, divided
2 tablespoons very strong black coffee
  (last night's pot will do very well)

On a trip to Santa Fe, my trail partner and I stopped for the night at a B&B just outside of Durango, Colorado. The woman who ran the place, Betty Nyland, had retired from ranching (by herself) up in the foothills and was tending tenderfoots who passed through. Instead of the usual granola in the morning, she served up a real ranch breakfast. Cholesterol was not in her vocabulary, nor was caffeine. She only knew how to do one thing—serve up a ranch-style breakfast and serve it well.

Heat the oil in a big iron skillet and fry the ham steaks until browned. Add 1/3 cup of the water, cover, lower the heat (or move the skillet to a cooler part of the cook fire, she said), and simmer the ham until tender, about 20 minutes. (This was when Betty whipped up the baking powder biscuits and made a fresh pot of equally strong black coffee.)

Take the ham out of the skillet and put it on a warm platter. Scrape the browned bits from the sides and bottom of the skillet and add the remaining water. (There should be about 1 cup in the skillet then.) Stir in the coffee, then pour it over the ham steaks.

Serves 4

"As a child I always had a fondness for adventure and outdoor exercise and especial fondness for horses which I began to ride at an early age and continued to do so until I became an expert rider being able to ride the most vicious and stubborn of horses, in fact the greater portion of my life in early times was spent in this manner."

—CALAMITY JANE (Martha Cannary Burke, 1852–1903)

Ranch House–Style Pork Chops

6 pork chops, sliced thick
Bacon fat
6 lemon slices, sliced thin
²/₃ cup homemade ketchup (see page 61)
2 tablespoons brown sugar
¹/₃ cup water

Brown the chops in bacon fat in a heavy skillet. Place a lemon slice on each chop.

Mix the ketchup, brown sugar, and water and pour over the chops. Cover and simmer for 30 minutes, basting the chops occasionally.

Serves 6

Connie Reeves was the oldest inductee of the Cowgirl Hall of Fame when she died at 101 after being thrown from her favorite horse, Dr. Pepper. She is credited as the one who admonished all Cowgirls, "Always saddle your own horse!"

"A Cowgirl needs only four animals in her life:

1. A 100x Beaver hat

2. A Ram in her garage

3. A good Horse

4. A Jackass to pay for it all."

—ANONYMOUS

Breakfast is an important part of the ranchers' and buckaroos' (be they man or woman) day. It gives them energy to ride for miles, mend fences, bring in snowbound cows and calves, and buck hay. Many present-day ranchers are from German stock, and many of their Old World recipes survive as ranch fare today.

Contrary to popular belief, beef is just a part of the diet on ranches. Pigs are easy to raise and give a lot of meat. There is always a plethora of ground pork after the hams and chops are cut and the bacon is cured and smoked. What to do with it? Serve this for breakfast and then saddle up!

Scrapple

1 pound ground pork sausage, seasoned with sage
2 cups yellow cornmeal
6 cups water
Salt and pepper to taste*
Bacon fat or vegetable oil

Pour the cornmeal into a saucepan and add 2 cups of water. Mix until smooth. Add the sausage and remaining 4 cups of water. Cover and cook on low heat until thick, about 25–30 minutes.

Pour mixture into 2 greased loaf pans (9x5x3) or 2 5-pound coffee cans, washed and rinsed. Cool. Cover and refrigerate overnight.

Remove scrapple from pan or can. Slice 1/3 inch thick and fry in a small amount of bacon fat or oil until brown and crisp around the edges.

Serve with molasses or maple syrup.

Serves 12. (Not serving a branding crew? Just cut the recipe in half and use 1 loaf pan or one coffee can. Serves 6)

*For you Cowgirls who like your grub hot, add a teaspoon of cayenne pepper, or to taste.

Main Dishes

Tad's Special

Barbara Inez (Tad) Lucas of Fort Worth, Texas, the youngest of twenty-four children, was considered one of the greatest professional Cowgirls of all time. She won all of the major trophies and titles available to rodeo Cowgirls from 1917 through the late 1920s. She was a fearless and innovative trick rider and toured in Wild West shows throughout the United States and Europe. She died in 1990, one of the last of the great Cowgirls.

1 pound ground beef
1 medium onion, chopped
1 cup cooked spinach, drained well and chopped fine
Salt to taste
2 eggs, beaten
Salt and pepper to taste
Tortillas or taco shells
1 cup grated Monterey Jack cheese

In a large skillet, brown the beef and onion. Stir in the spinach and salt. Simmer for 10 minutes.

Add the beaten eggs and stir fry with a fork until the eggs are set. Add the salt and pepper.

Place a large spoonful of mixture on or in a warm tortilla or taco shell. Top with a sprinkle of cheese and fold in half. You can go on and on with this by topping it off with

sour cream
guacamole
chopped black olives and/or
chopped chiles or peppers.

This dish is awfully good with flour tortillas or in taco shells. It is quick and easy and just the thing after a good ride on a mean bronc.

Serves 6

June's Ranch Beans

1 (16-ounce) can lima beans
2 (16-ounce) cans kidney beans
2 (16-ounce) cans garbanzo beans
4 (16-ounce) cans pork & beans
3/4 cup brown sugar
1/2 cup vinegar
1 cup tomato juice

Combine all ingredients in a big crock pot or slow cooker and cook on low, covered, for about 2 hours.

Variations: Add 1 pound ground beef or sausage cut into "moons" or diced leftover ham

Serves 10–12

Grandpa's Beans

John Leavitt asked me why he wasn't asked to be in this book. I told him it was because he is not a Cowgirl. He said, "Then you won't get to know about Grandpa's Beans." I gave in.

"Percy Leavitt was my dad's dad. He ranched outside of Boulder, Utah, the last place in the United States to have the U.S. Mail delivered by pack mule. His recipe is simple: For one person, cut up some bacon, put it in a pot, fry it crisp, then put in one can of pork and beans and lots of pepper. Heat and eat. For two people, two cans of beans and lots of pepper. For three people . . . you get the idea. Just be sure to put in lots of pepper."

June Kintzley Leavitt lives south of Lakeview, Oregon. The sky goes on forever in this remote section of southeastern Oregon. Pheasant, quail, chukker, grouse, deer, antelope, and elk abound, as do some pretty darned big cattle ranches. June has been the head Cowgirl behind the Double Arrow Ranch for many years. Her son, John, owns and operates Leavitts Western Wear in Sisters, Oregon. About this recipe June says, "Men really like it. I use it for branding crews and large groups at hunting season."

Black Bean Chili

2 tablespoons cooking oil
1 pound ground beef or beef cut into small chunks
1/2 cup chopped onion
2 (28-ounce) cans whole tomatoes with juice, crushed
2 (15- or 16-ounce) cans black beans, rinsed and drained
1 (4-ounce) can diced green chiles, mild, medium, or hot
1 tablespoon instant beef bouillon or beef base (1 cube)
1/4 teaspoon garlic powder
1 teaspoon cumin

In a Dutch oven, brown the beef in oil and drain.

Add the tomatoes, onions, chilies, bouillon and all the spices. Stir well. Heat to boiling, stirring often.

Reduce heat to low and simmer, covered, for 30 minutes, stirring occasionally.

Serves 6–8 hungry Cowgirls

Note:

If your chaps are getting a little tight, you can substitute the vegetable oil with vegetable spray and use ground turkey in place of beef. I don't know exactly how many calories you save by doing this, but you'll feel better about it.

"Sometimes we just have to put on our 'Big Girl Britches' and deal with it!"

 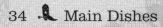

Joan's Chiles Rellenos

3 (7-ounce) cans whole green chiles

1 pound Monterey Jack cheese, grated

1 pound cheddar cheese, grated

3 eggs, beaten

3 tablespoons flour

1 (12-ounce) can evaporated milk

1 (15-ounce) can tomato sauce

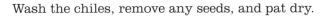

Wash the chiles, remove any seeds, and pat dry.

In a 9x13-inch baking pan, layer half of the chiles and then half of the cheeses. Repeat layers, reserving 1/2 cup of the cheese for topping.

In a medium bowl, beat the eggs. Add the flour and milk and beat until blended.

Pour the egg mixture over the chiles and cheese. The casserole can be refrigerated at this point while you go for a ride.

Bake at 350 degrees for 30 minutes. Spread the tomato sauce evenly over the top, sprinkle with the reserved cheese, and bake 15 minutes longer.

Cut into squares to serve.

Serves 6

Joan Triplett has been described as the "iron butterfly." No bigger than a minute, she has more energy per square ounce than most cowboys. Without a hair out of place, perfectly manicured nails, and an enthusiastic, adventuresome spirit, she is the quintessential Cowgirl in my eyes. To sit in front of a real log fire by her massive river rock fireplace is to enjoy what is the truest spirit of the West.

Rimrock Tomato Mac and Cheese

2 cups uncooked macaroni noodles
3 tablespoons butter
3 tablespoons flour
2 cups milk
2 cups shredded cheddar cheese
1/4 teaspoon salt
Fresh ground pepper to taste
2 ripe tomatoes, sliced
1/4 cup grated Parmesan cheese

Cook macaroni and drain. Set aside. Preheat oven to 350 degrees.

To make the sauce, melt butter in a saucepan. Blend in flour.
Cook and stir on medium heat for about 2 minutes, then add
the milk and stir constantly until it thickens. Stir in the cheddar
cheese and then the macaroni. Add salt and pepper to taste.
Mix well.

Pour macaroni and cheese into a baking dish. Arrange sliced
tomatoes on top and then sprinkle with Parmesan.

Bake uncovered 20–25 minutes or until bubbling and starting
to brown.

Serves 4

Cackleberries on Toast

3 tablespoons butter
2 tablespoons flour
1 teaspoon salt
2 cups warm milk
6 hard-boiled eggs
Salt and pepper to taste
8 slices toast

To make the white sauce, melt butter in a heavy saucepan. Add flour and salt and stir until well blended. Slowly add the warm milk, stirring constantly, until the sauce thickens. It will still be fairly thin.

Chop the egg whites and add them to the white sauce. Add the salt and pepper. Arrange slices of toast on a platter and pour the white sauce over them. Mash the egg yolks through a sieve and sprinkle on top.

Variation:
Add a slice of ham before pouring the egg sauce over the toast.

Serves 6

After Easter Casserole

1½ pounds cooked ham, sliced
3 pounds cooked yams or sweet potatoes, sliced
1 8-ounce (4 slices) can sliced pineapple, drained and cut in half
½ cup chopped pecans
¾ cup maple syrup

Preheat oven to 350 degrees. Arrange sliced ham, sliced potatoes, and pineapple alternately in a buttered casserole dish. Sprinkle the pecans on top.

Bake uncovered for 15 minutes. Remove from oven and pour the syrup over the casserole. Return to the oven and bake for 20 minutes more.

Serves 6

"My task in life is to be a happy woman."

—SALLY CONNERS, Montana horsewoman

SALADS *and* VEGETABLES

Lemon Lariat Apple Ring

2 packages lemon-flavored gelatin
3 cups hot water
6 tablespoons lemon juice
1½ cups red delicious apples, diced
1 cup celery, diced
½ cup coarsely broken walnuts
¼ cup mayonnaise
¼ cup sour cream

In a large bowl dissolve gelatin in hot water. Add lemon juice and chill until mixture begins to thicken. Fold in diced apples, celery, and nuts. Pour into an 8-inch round Jello mold. Chill until firm. Dress with a mixture of mayonnaise and sour cream.

Serves 6–8

Rio Brazos Salad

1 (15-ounce) can black beans, drained and rinsed

1 (16-ounce) can whole kernel corn, drained and rinsed

$1/2$ cup seeded and chopped red bell pepper

$1/2$ cup seeded and chopped green bell pepper

4 scallions, chopped (including the tops) or 1 small Vidalia
   or Walla Walla sweet onion, chopped

$1/4$ cup chopped celery

1 (4-ounce) can black olives, chopped

3 tablespoons lemon juice

2 tablespoons tomato salsa

1 tablespoon olive oil

Salt and pepper to taste

Sour cream

In a large bowl, combine beans, corn, peppers, scallions, celery, and olives.

In another bowl, stir together lemon juice, salsa, and olive oil. Combine the salsa mixture and bean mixture. Add more salsa to taste. Salt and pepper to taste. Refrigerate for at least 1 hour.

Top salad with dollops of sour cream.

Serves 6

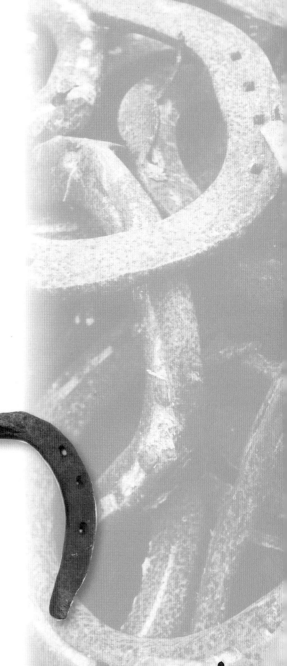

Cowgirl's Coleslaw

$\frac{1}{2}$ cup sour cream

$\frac{1}{4}$ cup mayonnaise

$\frac{1}{2}$ cup apple juice (or more to taste)

1 teaspoon dill weed (optional)

Salt and pepper to taste

3 cups thinly shredded cabbage (If you put the shredded cabbage in cold water in the icebox for about an hour and then drain well before making the coleslaw, the cabbage will be very crisp.)

2 tablespoons finely diced red onion

1 large tart-sweet apple, peeled and diced. Some of the best varieties to use are Braeburn, Gala, Gravenstein, Granny Smith, and Jonagold.

1 carrot, peeled and shredded

In a large salad bowl, combine sour cream, mayonnaise, apple juice, dill weed, and salt and pepper to taste. Mix the cabbage, onion, apple, and carrot into the sauce. Refrigerate for at least 4 hours to allow the ingredients to blend.

Serves 6

Montana Cowgirl Fannie Sperry Steele turned her love of horses into a rodeo career that included being named World Champion bronc rider as well as appearing as a sharpshooter. She went on to form her own Wild West show and toured the country. She retired from the rodeo and went home to Montana to open a guest ranch. She personally guided her guests into the Rocky Mountains until she was seventy-five years old.

Sharie's Sauerkraut Salad

For the salad:

4 cups sauerkraut, drained
1 8-ounce can garbanzo beans
1 cup chopped celery
1 cup shredded carrots
1 small onion, diced
1 4-ounce jar pimentos, diced (optional)
1 red or green bell pepper, diced (optional)

For the dressing:

1/2 cup vegetable oil
1 cup white sugar
1 cup rice vinegar
Poppy seeds, about 1/2 cup
Pepper to taste

Combine all the salad ingredients in a large salad bowl.
Mix and refrigerate.

In another bowl, combine all the dressing ingredients. Mix well.

Toss the dressing with the salad ingredients just before serving.

Serves 12–16

Sharie Forde of Sisters, Oregon, loves to compete in team penning and sorting—both noisy, not to mention fast-paced, events. She is too modest to say just how many trophy buckles she has won. (Hint: quite a few.) She says, "The best food is something someone else has cooked." But she does offer this piquant salad, which is wonderful for potluck suppers following a penning.

"The Cowgirl faces life head on, lives by her own lights and makes no excuses."

—DALE EVANS, the Queen of the Cowgirls

Tamarack Baked Carrots

24 large carrots, peeled and sliced
$1/2$ cup butter
$1/2$ cup brown sugar, packed
$1/2$ teaspoon baking powder
2 eggs, beaten
1 cup evaporated milk
Salt and pepper to taste
$1/4$ cup bread crumbs

Running a girl's camp can be fraught with peril—not the least of which is providing the campers with a healthy diet. Tamarack campers were well fed three times a day, nutrition slipped in a variety of ways. Most girls ages nine to seventeen don't like and won't eat carrots. They would rather feed them to their horses. They always ate this up at dinner! I can personally attest to this fact.

Boil the carrots until they are "al dente" or nearly done. Drain.

Preheat oven to 350 degrees. Add the butter to the cooked carrots, then mash them. Stir in the remaining ingredients except the bread crumbs and mix well.

Pour carrots into a greased casserole dish. Sprinkle on the bread crumbs and bake for 30 minutes or until the bread crumbs are browned.

Serves 8 (but doubles well to serve 16)

Kentucky Corn Pudding

3 tablespoons butter, room temperature
2 tablespoons sugar
2 tablespoons flour
1 teaspoon salt
3 eggs
2 cups fresh, frozen, or canned (drained) corn kernels,
  coarsely chopped
1½ cups half-and-half or heavy cream

Preheat the oven to 350 degrees. In a buttered 1½ quart casserole dish, mix the butter, sugar, flour, and salt. Beat in the eggs, and stir in the corn and cream.

Bake for 45 minutes until slightly puffed and brown.

Serves 6

Judy Santille has a battered recipe box filled to overflowing with tried-and-true recipes sure to please a crew of cowboys or guests at her Hotel Diamond table. Most of the recipes are in her head. When it's time for supper, she simply looks into her pantry to see what's on hand and goes to work. In late summer there is nearly always fresh corn. In mid-winter canned corn is on the shelves. Either one will do for this hot and tasty dish.

GENERAL STORE

Santa Fe Vegetables

Georgia O'Keeffe has to be considered a Cowgirl. She is, after all, an inductee into the National Cowgirl Hall of Fame. Her spirit and style, reflected in her paintings and watercolors done in and around Santa Fe, embody a true West in vivid and dramatic color. I made a pilgrimage to Santa Fe to visit the newly opened Georgia O'Keeffe Museum. There is a vegetarian cafe nearby that serves this wonderful combination of tasty vegetables. O'Keeffe would have loved them and, quite possibly, would have painted them for their riot of colors.

2 tablespoons vegetable oil
2 cups chopped onion
2 cloves garlic, minced
3 carrots, cut into half-moons
1 large zucchini, cut into half moons
1 green pepper, seeded and diced
2 cups fresh corn kernels
2 cups chopped and drained fresh, ripe tomatoes
1 teaspoon cumin
1 teaspoon coriander
1 tablespoon chopped cilantro
Salt and pepper to taste
Sour cream, dollop per serving

Heat oil in a large skillet. Sauté the onion and garlic for about 5 minutes. Add the carrots. Cover the skillet and sauté for an additional 5 minutes, stirring occasionally.

Stir in the remaining vegetables and the seasonings and cook on low heat just until the vegetables are tender.

Serve open-face on cornbread or in a pita pocket. Top with sour cream.

Serves 8

"Where I was born and where and how I have lived is unimportant. It is what I have done with where I have been that should be of interest."

—GEORGIA O'KEEFFE, 1887–1986

soups and stews

High Desert Potato and Bacon Soup

Many women out on the plains and deserts had to "make do" with what was at hand and come up with satisfying meals. All the ingredients in this soup are "to hand" (as they used to say), and it is very satisfying! This recipe comes from a shepherd's daughter who spent the first six years of her life in a covered wagon following a vast herd of sheep over the hills of the High Desert of Central Oregon.

3 large potatoes, peeled and cubed
1 medium onion, peeled and cubed
1 quart water
Salt and pepper to taste
5 strips bacon
1½ cups bread crumbs from stale bread
½ cup cream (evaporated milk will do)

Cook the potatoes and onion in water until soft. "Mash" them a little bit to release more flavor, but do not drain. Add salt and pepper to taste.

Cut the bacon into small pieces and fry until crisp and brown. Remove the bacon from the fat to drain. Add the bread crumbs to the fat and stir and toast until brown.

Add the cooked bacon and browned bread crumbs to the potato and onion soup and reheat, adding more seasonings if you wish. Stir in the cream or milk.

Serves 6

Kate's Chicken and White Bean Soup

1 pound white (Great Northern) beans
1–2 tablespoons canola or other cooking oil
1 small onion, sliced into thin strips
1 fresh jalapeno pepper, seeded and finely chopped
1.5 pounds skinless, boneless chicken thighs,
    cut into 1/2-inch pieces
8–10 cups rich chicken broth
Salt and pepper to taste
Dash Tabasco sauce

Clean, rinse, and soak beans for at least 4 hours, preferably overnight. Drain and discard bean water.

Heat oil in a large Dutch oven or heavy pot. Sauté the onion over medium heat, stirring occasionally. When onions become transparent and are just barely browning, add jalapeno pepper. Sauté until fragrant. Add chicken and sauté until chicken releases juices and begins to brown. Add beans and chicken broth. Bring to a gentle boil, then turn down to low and simmer, covered, until beans are tender, about 2 hours.

Check liquid level after 1 hour; if it seems low, add a little more broth. Taste and correct seasoning with salt and pepper, if necessary.

Serve hot with a dash of Tabasco sauce.

Serves 6–8

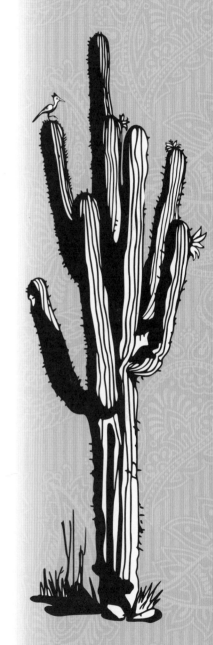

Fit for a Queen Green Chili Soup

½ cup vegetable oil

2 pounds lean pork loin, cut into 1/2-inch cubes

1 cup flour, mixed with salt and pepper to taste
   for dredging the pork

2 tablespoons minced garlic

2 cups diced onions

3 cups diced tomatoes

2 cups canned green chiles, seeded and diced

1 cup tomato juice

1 cup water

1 tablespoon Tabasco sauce

1 tablespoon coriander

Salt and pepper to taste

In a large skillet or Dutch oven, heat the oil.

Dredge the meat in the flour until well coated. Add to the heated oil and brown on all sides.

Add the garlic and onion to the meat and simmer until the onions are tender. Stir often, getting all the bits from the bottom of the pan.

Add the tomatoes, chiles, tomato juice, water, Tabasco sauce, and coriander. Simmer until the meat is tender, about one hour. Add salt and pepper if necessary.

Serves 6–8

Beef Stew. Period.

1/3 cup flour
Salt and pepper to taste
2 pounds beef stew meat, cubed
1/4 cup shortening
1 tablespoon lemon juice
1 tablespoon Worcestershire sauce
2 bay leaves, torn into pieces
12 carrots, chopped into moons
1 large onion, sliced
8 potatoes, peeled and cubed

Mix the flour, salt, and pepper on a plate and dredge the beef cubes in it. Shake off the excess flour.

Melt the shortening in a cast-iron Dutch oven or heavy pot with a cover. Put the beef, 5–6 pieces at a time, in the hot shortening and brown on all sides. Remove the beef cubes and drain on a paper towel. Continue until all the beef is browned and dark.

Put all the beef back into the pot and cover with 4 cups boiling water. (Be careful of the "splatter.")

Stir in the lemon juice, Worcestershire sauce, and bay leaves.

Reduce heat to low, cover, and simmer for 1 1/2–2 hours, or until the meat is very tender, stirring now and then.

Add the carrots, onion slices, and potatoes and cook for 20–25 minutes until the potatoes can be pierced with a fork.

Serves 6–8

There are as many recipes for stew as there are colors of horses. This one is the basic, the basis for any and all variations you care to add or subtract. It is rich, dark brown, and satisfying. It is my mother's recipe. Bay leaves were a part of her life. You can ignore them if you wish, but the stew is better for them, I think. Mother was not a Cowgirl, and I believe she worried that I would become one. Mother, I did. But I always have bay leaves handy.

Branding Stew

1½ pounds hamburger

4 potatoes (more or less), peeled
and sliced

2 carrots, peeled and diced

1 large onion, peeled and chopped

Salt and pepper to taste

Link sausage, cooked and cut into
bite-size pieces

1 pound grated sharp cheddar cheese

Brown the hamburger in a large, heavy skillet. Add the potatoes, carrots, onion, and a little bit of water (¼ cup) and cover. Cook on medium heat until the vegetables are soft, stirring now and then. Add seasonings to taste.

Stir in the sausage and sprinkle the grated cheese on top of the mix. Cover again and heat until the cheese is melted.

Serves 4

> "If I had it all to do over again, what would I do different? Be just a little bit wilder— ride more wild horses."
>
> —MARTHA STRANAHAN, early-day Central Oregon horsewoman

Monday Night Stew Pie

1 pound bacon

1–2 pounds leftover chicken, turkey, roast beef, or lamb, cut into bite-size pieces

32 ounces (about 4 cups) leftover vegetables—carrots, string beans, or onions—chopped (Add a small can of corn or green peas if you are short on vegetables.)

Leftover gravy, if available

2 cups leftover mashed potatoes

1 cup of shredded cheddar cheese

Cut the bacon into 1-inch pieces and fry in a large skillet until crisp. Drain off the fat. Add the meat and stir over medium heat. Mix in the vegetables. Add leftover gravy, if you have it, and stir it in.

Preheat oven to 350 degrees. Transfer the meat and vegetables to a lightly greased 10-inch baking dish. Spoon the mashed potatoes over the top, spreading to the edges. Then sprinkle the grated cheese all over the top.

Bake for about 10 minutes, or until the pie starts to bubble.

Serves 6

Relishes,
Salsas,
Sauces&
Ketchups

Green Tomato Relish

Out in the West on the High Desert, and up on the flanks of the mountains, the summers are short but sweet. Those who have planted a vegetable garden usually wind up with lots of tomatoes that didn't ripen. What to do with them is this old standby recipe that dates back to the pioneer days. Salsas came later. This relish was first. A jar of it is always on the dinner table in the ranch house. It is wonderful with hamburgers, chicken, or scrambled eggs.

18 cups green tomatoes, diced and drained
2 large Walla Walla sweet onions, chopped fine
1 red pepper, seeded and chopped fine
1 green pepper, seeded and chopped fine
3 cups vinegar
9 cups sugar
3 tablespoons coarse salt
1 teaspoon each: allspice and cloves
2 tablespoons each: cinnamon and nutmeg

Combine all the ingredients in a heavy pot and cook slowly, stirring often, until the relish reaches a good, thick consistency. Pack into sterile jars and seal. Process in a hot water bath for 25 minutes.

This will give you about ten 8-ounce jars for the pantry.

Cowgirl Crude Salsa

3 ripe tomatoes, chopped
1/4–1/2 cup minced hot peppers (fresh or canned)
1/2 cup finely chopped onion
Tabasco or other hot sauce to taste
Salt and pepper to taste
3/4 cup chopped Spanish olives (optional)

Combine all the ingredients. Refrigerate at least 1 hour before serving.

Store in the refrigerator for up to 1 week.

Makes about 2 cups

For those of you who insist that it isn't Western if there isn't a salsa, here it is. Cowgirls don't have a lot of time to spend fussing, so a "crude" tomato hot sauce has a clean and fresh taste. Depending on the amount and kind of peppers and chiles used, the intensity of hotness can range from mild to volcanic. This Texas-style salsa tastes best at room temperature, so take it out of the fridge at least an hour before you use it for dipping corn chips, as a topping for frittatas, or as a condiment in any Mexican entree. Olé!

Mary Ann (Molly) Goodnight (1839–1926) was the wife of Texas cattleman Charles Goodnight. Molly drove supply wagons and took charge of ranch operations when her husband was absent. Affectionately called "the little mother of the plains," she cared for the cowhands and Indians who came to the ranch as a way to combat the loneliness of being the only woman in the area.

Fruity Salsa

2 kiwi, peeled and chopped

1 cup any melon, chopped

1/2 cup fresh pineapple, chopped

3 or 4 tablespoons red onion, finely chopped

2 tablespoons lime juice

1/2 jalapeno pepper (or more if you like it hot), chopped fine

1/4 teaspoon salt

1 1/2 tablespoons chopped cilantro

1 tablespoon olive oil

Pepper to taste

In a medium bowl, combine all ingredients. Adjust flavors to taste. Cover and refrigerate for 3 hours or overnight. You can substitute any kind of tropical fruit—it all works.

Makes about 2 cups

"I wonder if all women spend their time cooking, sewing and tending their chickens and pigs."

—SARA BROWN, 1900, Wenatchee, Washington

Out of Your Garden
Tomato Ketchup

1 gallon tomatoes, peeled and chopped

1 quart white vinegar

1 quart white sugar

$1/2$ teaspoon red pepper

1 teaspoon allspice

$1/2$ teaspoon black pepper

1 tablespoon salt

Crush the tomatoes through a sieve directly into a large saucepan. Add the rest of the ingredients and cook slowly until desired thickness. Place into hot, sterilized jars and seal.

Makes approximately 4 cups

The Cowgirls CODE OF THE WEST

Always tighten your cinch.

Keep your gear in order.

Always saddle your own horse!

Always take care of your horse before you take care of yourself.

Laugh at life's little stampedes.

Gallop for cover with the big ones.

Whatever you do, do it the best you can.

When a Cowgirl is about to leave the chutes for a wild ride on a bucking bronc, lean over and whisper to her, "Don't weaken!"

Ride on, Cowgirl!

Keepin' It Simple Bar-B-Que Sauce

The Cowgirl most responsible for bringing back to life the Cowgirls of the past is Polly Helm, originally from Pendleton, Oregon, home of the world-famous Pendleton Round-Up. She discovered a photo of Kitty Canutt (titled "Champion of All") and started collecting other images and information of "lady buckaroos." In 1986 she put it all together in the form of the Pendleton Cowgirl Company, which produces calendars, note cards, magnets, and more that feature an old print on the front and its story on the back.

Polly says, "The cowgirl spirit is a state of mind and heart. The mystique is built around the idea of women doing what they love to do, despite the risks involved. It's about being true to oneself."

Her recipe for barbecue sauce is simple. Here it is in her words:

"Equal parts ketchup, mustard, dark molasses and Worcestershire sauce. Nothin' fancy, but always a favorite at our annual summer rib fest."

Kitty Wilks Canutt was a professional bronc rider and the All-Around Champion Cowgirl at the 1916 Pendleton Round-Up in Pendleton, Oregon, for her bucking horse and relay-race events. It was at this rodeo that she met and married Yakima Canutt, a winner of the title "All-Around Cowboy" at the Pendleton Round-Up in 1917, 1919, 1920, and 1923. They were divorced in 1919.

Kitty was known as the "Diamond Girl" or "Diamond Kitty," because she had a diamond set in her front tooth. She would occasionally remove and pawn the diamond when she needed contest entry money.

Desserts
and Sweets

Tamarack Tea Cakes

1 cup soft butter
6 tablespoons powdered sugar
1 teaspoon vanilla
2 cups cake flour
1 cup chopped pecans
Powdered sugar for rolling

Preheat oven to 350 degrees. Using a wooden spoon, cream the butter and powdered sugar in a large bowl until well blended. Add the vanilla and mix again. Add the flour and the pecans. Mix well.

Roll dough into balls about the size of a ping-pong ball. Place these on an ungreased cookie sheet and bake until golden, about 8 minutes. Watch that they don't burn.

Roll warm tea cakes in powdered sugar and place on waxed paper to cool and dry.

Makes about 36 tea cakes

For many girls aged nine to seventeen, a four-week session at Camp Tamarack, on the shores of Dark Lake in central Oregon, was the turning point in their lives.

Not only did they get to ride horseback through the fragrant pines all day long, swim and canoe in and on the crystal-clear waters of Dark Lake, and sleep under the tents on starry nights following the evening campfire and "Taps" played by a bugler at the foot of the flagpole each and every night, but they came under the spell of the owner, founder, and director, Donna Gill.

From the beginning, the program was innovative. Activities took place at all times. The emphasis was on horseback riding, swimming, boating, crafts, and the indefinable quality of being a "good scout," Donna's highest praise.

She instilled in the Tamarackers a set of standards and taught them to accept responsibility. Her rule was that no girl should ever do anything that would endanger another person or cause unhappiness.

At the end of each session, July and August, parents were invited for a special display of mounted drills, swimming and diving exhibitions, archery, and crafts. A gala luncheon was served with the traditional Tamarack Tea Cakes for dessert.

Donna died in 1983. But her spirit lives on in women who still strive to be "good scouts."

Sour Cream and Raisin Pie

Following her stint at the ZX Ranch, Judy Santille ran the Diamond Hotel in Diamond, Oregon. An out-of-the way place, rich in the history of the "Oregon outback" (as south-central Oregon is known), Judy brought her culinary skills that she learned on the High Desert to the long tables for her guests to enjoy. A favorite is this pie.

10-inch pie shell, prebaked
5 eggs
2½ cups sour cream
¾ cup sugar
2 teaspoons vanilla
¼ teaspoon salt
¼ teaspoon nutmeg
1½ cup raisins

Preheat the oven to 350 degrees. Lightly beat the eggs in a medium bowl. Fold in the sour cream, sugar, vanilla, salt, nutmeg, and raisins.

Pour filling into the pie shell and bake for about 1 hour or until set.

Makes ten small slices or six large slices

"And let us consider how we may spur one another on toward love and good deeds."

—HEBREWS 10 24 NIV

Leather Cookies

3/4 cup shortening

2 cups sugar, divided

1 egg, beaten well

1/4 cup molasses

1/2 teaspoon salt

2 teaspoons baking soda

1 teaspoon ground clove

1 teaspoon ground ginger

2 cups flour

1 cup raisins

Preheat oven to 350 degrees. In a large bowl, cream the shortening, 1 cup of sugar, and egg. Add molasses, salt, baking soda, spices, flour, and raisins.

Form dough into balls about the size of a walnut. Roll in the remaining sugar and place on an ungreased cookie sheet. Don't flatten—they do that all by themselves.

Bake cookies for 8–10 minutes. Do not over bake. They should be chewy when cool. The resemblance of these good cookies to well-worn leather is startling. Don't let appearances fool you: Like good leather, you can rely on these.

Makes about 4 dozen cookies

The Women's Professional Rodeo Association (WPRA), formed in 1948 by twenty-eight women rodeo riders, is the oldest organization of female professional athletes in the United States and the only one controlled and managed entirely by women.

Liz's Crummy Coffee Cake

2⅔ cups brown sugar
4 cups unsifted flour
1 cup margarine
1 pint sour cream
1 pound raisins
1 cup nuts (walnuts are preferred)

If you check out the Walt Disney film *Run, Appaloosa, Run!*, you will see a girl jumping an Appaloosa horse over a touring car. That girl (who was the stunt rider and stand-in for the star of the movie) is now a woman, Elizabeth "Liz" Dixon. She has been riding and jumping throughout her life, and I think she would jump a horse over a car even today. She has real Cowgirl spirit.

Preheat oven to 350 degrees. Combine brown sugar, flour, and margarine in a medium bowl. With your hands (wash them first after riding, Liz cautions!), crumble all until it is . . . well, crumbly.

Remove ½ cup of the crumbles and set aside.

To the mixture remaining in the bowl, add sour cream, raisins, and nuts. Stir and blend well.

Pour batter into an 8 × 8 buttered ovenproof dish. Top with reserved crumbles. Bake for 80 minutes.

Serve warm with strong black coffee.

Serves 4–6

Mustang Chocolate Cake

1 1/2 cups flour
3 tablespoons dark cocoa
1 teaspoon baking soda
1 cup sugar
1/2 teaspoon salt
5 tablespoons cooking oil
1 tablespoon vinegar
1 teaspoon vanilla
1 cup cold water

Preheat oven to 350 degrees. Sift the flour, cocoa, baking soda, sugar, and salt into a greased 9x9-inch square cake pan.

Using the end of a wooden spoon, or your index finger, make three holes in the dry mixture. Into one, pour the cooking oil; into the second, the vinegar; into the third, the vanilla. Pour the cold water slowly over the whole thing. Then beat it with a fork until it's almost smooth and you can no longer see the dry ingredients. Be sure to get into the corners.

Bake for 30 minutes. Serve straight from the pan.

Makes about 12 squares

Like the mustangs that roam the West, no one seems to know where this cake came from. And, like those hardy horses, this recipe is a mixture of odd things that all add up to something wonderful. It's the best chocolate cake you will ever make. It travels to potlucks, campouts, and picnics very well and doesn't even need frosting.

Wild Horse Annie was born Velma Brown on March 5, 1912, in Reno, Nevada. She became an advocate for the wild mustangs that were being rounded up and slaughtered. Velma was sarcastically nicknamed "Wild Horse Annie" by one of her bitterest opponents, Dan Solari, who went on to become an employee of the Montana Bureau of Land Management (BLM).

One of the most unique letters of support Annie received was from a tribal chief of the Sioux Indians. He offered to bring a band of armed warriors to assist her. On December 15, 1971, Annie's efforts paid off and Congress unanimously passed the Free-Roaming Wild Horse and Burro Act.

While the women who moved west in the pioneer days could not be called "Cowgirls," they were nevertheless cut from the same cloth. They were tough and resilient and could whip up delicious things with one hand while tending the garden, babies, animals, and what-have you with the other. I got this recipe from Rae Pursley, a one-generation-removed descendant of the pioneers who settled in Aurora, Oregon, in the 1860s.

"Ranch women are as sharp as nails and just as hard. If Eve had been a ranch woman, she would never have tempted Adam with an apple. She would have ordered him to make his meal himself."

—ANTHONY TROLLOPE, 1862

Raw Apple Cake

4 cups diced apples (Granny Smith, Gravenstein, or Gala are good)

$1/2$ cup cooking oil

2 cups sugar

2 eggs, well beaten

1 cup chopped nuts

1 cup seedless raisins

2 teaspoons vanilla

1 tablespoon vinegar

2 cups flour

2 teaspoons cinnamon

2 teaspoons baking soda

1 teaspoon salt

Preheat oven to 325 degrees. In a large bowl, mix apples, oil, sugar, eggs, nuts, raisins, vanilla, and vinegar.

In a separate bowl, sift together flour, cinnamon, baking soda, and salt.

Add the dry ingredients to the apple mixture. Pour into a greased 9x13-inch pan and bake for 1 hour.

Serves 8–10

Texas Two-Step Blackberry Dumplings

Step One:

2 pints fresh blackberries, washed

3/4 cup water

1 cup sugar

1 1/2 tablespoons butter, softened

Combine all the ingredients in a large saucepan and simmer while preparing the dough, below.

Step Two:

2 cups flour

3 tablespoons sugar

1/2 teaspoon salt

3 1/2 tablespoons baking powder

1 egg

3/4 cup milk

Sift the flour, sugar, salt, and baking powder into a mixing bowl. Add the egg and mix well. Add the milk to make a stiff batter.

Bring the berry mixture back to a boil. Drop the dumpling batter, a large spoonful at a time, into the boiling mixture. Do not crowd the dumplings—be sure they have room to expand as they cook.

Cover and cook for 20 minutes. Lift out with a slotted spoon.

These dumplings are good hot with ice cream or cold for breakfast. If you don't have blackberries, you can use Marion berries, raspberries, blueberries, or ripe peaches.

Makes about 8 dumplings

Kickin' Apple Pie Enchiladas

2 tablespoons cornstarch

2 tablespoons water

2 cups apple juice or apple cider (sweetened)

5 medium tart apples (Jonagolds, Gravenstein, Gala or Braeburn)

1 tablespoon lemon juice

1 chipotle pepper in adobo sauce (these come packed several to
a 7-ounce can, but you only need 1 for a fiery kick.)

2 teaspoons butter

1/4 cup sugar

1 1/2 teaspoon cinnamon

10 (6-inch) flour tortillas

Additional sugar and cinnamon

Combine cornstarch and water in a small container and stir until dissolved. Pour the cornstarch mixture and apple cider into a saucepan and heat to boiling over medium-high heat, stirring constantly. When the mixture begins to thicken, allow it to boil another 30 seconds, remove from heat, cover, and set aside.

Core, peel, and dice apples so that you have about 5 cups. Place apple cubes in cold water with the lemon juice to prevent them from browning.

Seed and chop the chipotle peppers.

In a sauté pan, melt the butter. Drain the apples and add them to the pan. Cook over medium heat until apples begin to soften, about 5–7 minutes. Then stir in cinnamon, 1/2 teaspoon chipotle pepper (less if you want it mild, more if you like it hot), and about 1/2 cup of the apple cider sauce. Cook another 3–5 minutes. Remove from heat and set aside for assembly of enchiladas.

Sometimes a gal has to vary it, or, as Emeril would say, "Kick it up a notch." This is not your mother's apple pie. This is my sister Robin's invention, and she doesn't even own a pair of boots.

Preheat oven to 350 degrees.

To assemble the enchiladas, place about ¼ cup of the apple cube mixture in the middle of a 6-inch tortilla. Roll up and place in a well-buttered 7x11-inch baking dish, seam side down (8-inch square baking dish will also work, but it will only hold about 8 enchiladas). Repeat with remaining tortillas, setting them side by side in the pan.

Pour remaining apple cider sauce and any remaining apple mixture over the enchiladas. Sprinkle with additional sugar and cinnamon and bake for 25–30 minutes, or until the sauce is bubbling and the enchiladas are beginning to brown.

Serve with sharp cheddar cheese and vanilla ice cream.

Serves 4–6

Boiled Puddin' with Whiskey or Rum Sauce

2 cups flour

2 cups soft bread crumbs

½ cup packed brown sugar

1 tablespoon baking soda

1 teaspoon salt

1 teaspoon cinnamon

⅛ teaspoon ground cloves

¼ teaspoon ground nutmeg

1 cup raisins or peeled and diced apples

1 cup ground suet or 1/3 cup olive oil

½ cup chopped nuts

⅔ cup evaporated milk

½ cup light molasses

In mixing bowl, combine flour, bread crumbs, brown sugar, baking soda, salt, cinnamon, cloves, and nutmeg. Stir in raisins or apples, oil or suet, and nuts.

Stir in milk and molasses and mix well.

Place the pudding in a cotton sack or cotton dish towel and tie the top closed. Boil water in a pan deep enough to cover the sack. Cover and boil gently for 2 hours. Turn puddin', rounded side up, on a plate and let stand for 30 minutes or more before serving.

Serves 6–8

Whiskey or Rum Sauce

1 cup butter
1 cup sugar
1 cup evaporated milk or 1 cup half and half
¼ cup whiskey, brandy, or rum

Melt butter in cast iron skillet over medium heat. Stir in sugar and continue stirring until sugar dissolves.

Gradually stir in milk and bring to a boil. Stir over medium heat 10–12 minutes, or until mixture becomes a smooth, medium-thick sauce.

Remove sauce from heat and stir in whiskey, brandy, or rum.

Serve warm over Boiled Puddin'. And slice the puddin' like you would quarter an apple, remembering that it is very rich.

Makes about 2 cups

"Cowgirl is an attitude, really. A pioneer spirit, a special American brand of courage. The cowgirl faces life head on, lives by her own lights, and makes no excuses. Cowgirls take stands. They speak up. They defend the things they hold dear. A cowgirl might be a rancher, or a barrel racer, or a bull rider, or an actress. But she's just as likely to be a checker at the local Winn Dixie, a full-time mother, a banker, an attorney, or an astronaut."

—DALE EVANS ROGERS, "The Queen of the Cowgirls," Los Angeles, 1992

Maple-Flavored Gingerbread

2½ cups sifted flour

1½ teaspoons baking soda

1 teaspoon ground cinnamon

1 teaspoon ground ginger

½ teaspoon ground cloves

½ teaspoon salt

½ cup shortening

½ cup sugar

1 egg

½ cup molasses

½ cup maple syrup

1 cup hot water

Preheat oven to 350 degrees. In a small bowl, sift together the flour, baking soda, cinnamon, ginger, cloves, and salt.

In a large bowl, cream together the shortening and sugar until light and fluffy. Add the egg and beat well. Gradually beat in the molasses and maple syrup.

Add the dry ingredients to the wet alternately with the water mixture, beating well after each addition. Pour batter into a lightly buttered 8-inch square baking dish.

Bake 40 minutes or until cake tests done. Cool in pan on a rack.

Serves 12

Cowgirl Fudge

3 (6-ounce) packages semi-sweet chocolate chips
1 (14-ounce) can sweetened condensed milk (not evaporated!)
Salt to taste
3/4 cup chopped nuts
1 teaspoon vanilla

In a heavy saucepan, melt the chocolate chips, milk, and salt.
Stir constantly and keep the heat low to prevent burning.
Remove from the heat and stir in the nuts and vanilla.

Spread fudge into a wax paper–lined 8-inch square pan.
Chill 2 hours or until firm.

Turn the fudge out onto a cutting board and peel off the paper.
Cut into squares.

Makes about 2 pounds

Cowgirls may not agree on
the answers to all questions.
For example, just how much
fringe is too much fringe?
(Answer: You can never
have enough fringe.) Or,
are paint horses superior
to plain-colored horses?
(Answer: Paints rule!) But
Cowgirls all agree on fudge.

Fancy Mints

Even Cowgirls now and then have to come up with something for a wedding, shower, or birthday celebration. These mints are easy, good to eat, and fancy!

¹/₂ pound butter
1lb. package, (16-ounces) powdered sugar,
    reserving ¹/₈ of a cup for dipping
1 tablespoon heavy cream
Oil of peppermint or peppermint extract
Food coloring

Cream the butter in a large mixing bowl and then add the powdered sugar ¹/₂ cup at a time. Add the heavy cream slowly and beat thoroughly after each addition. Add peppermint extract, one drop at a time, to taste.

Divide the mixture into however many colors you wish for your fancy mints. Select a color and add one scant drop of the coloring until the color that you want is reached. For a pale pink, add a small amount of red; yellow for buttercup yellow; yellow and green for mint color; and a tiny amount of blue for sky blue.

Roll mints into small balls, place on parchment paper, and press with a fork that has been dipped in powdered sugar. Let set over night.

Makes about 36 candies

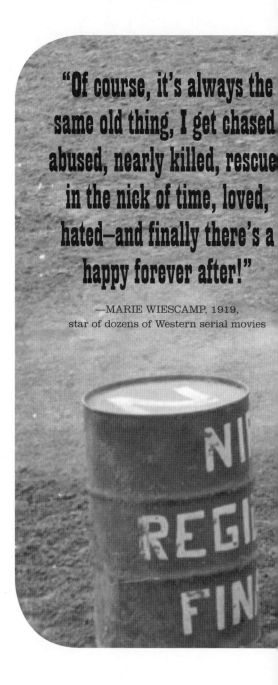

"Of course, it's always the same old thing, I get chased, abused, nearly killed, rescued in the nick of time, loved, hated—and finally there's a happy forever after!"

—MARIE WIESCAMP, 1919,
star of dozens of Western serial movies

Goober Candies

1 egg
1 tablespoon butter, softened
1/4 teaspoon salt
1/2 teaspoon vanilla
1/2 cup peanut butter
1 cup powdered sugar
Chopped peanuts, about 1 cup

Combine and beat together the egg, butter, salt, vanilla, and peanut butter. Stir in enough powdered sugar to make the mixture firm enough to handle. Shape into small balls—big enough for a "two-bite" candy. Roll each ball in chopped peanuts. Place on waxed paper and then refrigerate to set. These keep well in an airtight container.

Makes about 36 candies

"Someday,
I'll marry a cowboy
But first,
I want to be one."

—ANONYMOUS

Jams AND Jellies

PENDLETON OREGON. 191

Bertha Blancett's Quince Jelly

Quince is a golden or greenish yellow fruit. Hard and apple shaped, it grows on a small, thorny bush related to the rose family. The five-petal flowers range from deep red to pale salmon. Because they are so hardy, the quince bush is always a staple in pioneer homesteads.

Scrub and cut quince into quarters. Remove the seeds. Place in a saucepan and add enough water to cover the fruit. Cover the pan and cook until soft. Drain, then force through a sieve.

To 3 cups of quince pulp, add 3–4 cups of sugar. Cook until thick and smooth, about 20 minutes. Stir frequently, as it will want to stick.

Put into hot, sterilized jars.

Makes 3 cups

Bertha Kaepernick Blancett was the quintessential Cowgirl. As a young girl she would ride her saddle horse over the hills to the local rodeos, leading her bucking horse. She'd climb aboard and ride it out to the whistle. She competed against men, and she nearly always took home the prize-money.

An All-Around Cowgirl at the Pendleton Round-Up from 1911–1918, Blancett won the Cowgirls bucking contest many times, as well as trick-riding and relay-racing contests.

Blancett married a cowboy named Del. Her German heritage never left her, and she was as adept in the kitchen as she was in the corrals.

In 1999 Blancett was inducted into the National Cowgirl Hall of Fame due to the efforts of my friend Joanna Stewart, herself a Cowgirl and daughter of Andy Herregia, noted stock contractor. Bertha lived her last years on the Herregia Ranch in southern California, and Joanna followed her around and learned quite a few things. One of them was how to make this unusual jelly.

Rose Petal Jelly

2 cups fresh rose petals (It goes without saying that
  pesticide- and herbicide-free petals pulled from the
  flowers should be used.)
1 1/2 cups boiling water
2 tablespoons lemon juice
3 cups granulated sugar
3 ounces liquid pectin

Rinse the rose petals in cool water and drain. Place petals in a
large bowl and pour the boiling water over them. Allow them to
stand 24 hours to leach the color and flavor.

Strain the liquid into a 4-quart pot, discarding the petals.

Add lemon juice and sugar to the liquid. Stir to dissolve the sugar.
Bring to a boil over high heat. Stir in the pectin and continue to
cook and stir until the jelly comes to a rolling boil that cannot be
stirred down. Boil for an additional minute. Remove from heat.

Use a metal spoon to skim off the foam. Ladle the hot jelly into
hot, sterilized jars, leaving 1/4-inch head space. Screw the sterile
lids on tight and process in a boiling water canner for 10 minutes (15 minutes at 1,000 feet, 20 minutes above 6,000 feet).

Makes 3 half-pints

*"While I'm cooking, or dish washing,
I keep my head filled with
beautiful dreams."*

—VERA RAINS, 1901 Butte, Montana

Along with the quince
bush, women who lived
on remote ranches
tried their best to have
something pretty in the
garden along with the
standard vegetables and
fruits. A rose bush was
"pretty" and was usually
an old-fashioned and
hardy variety. No hybrid
teas for these gritty
gardeners!

The old-fashioned
roses have an abundance
of petals and are sweetly
scented. Deer love roses,
so it was always a battle
each year to have a few
blooms to put in a jam
jar on the windowsill.
The petals could also
be gathered and made
into a potpourri as well
as a very feminine jelly
to serve with biscuits if
another ranch wife came
to call.

Tea was spooned out
of the tin and brewed
in the teapot, and then
the ladies could settle
down and discuss the
price of cattle, the recent
snowstorm, and the
pending birth of foals
and calves.

Oregon Grape Jelly

8 cups ripe Oregon grape berries
1½ cups sugar per cup berry juice

The state flower of Oregon, and found throughout the West from British Columbia to California in the mountains, Oregon grape (also known as the holly grape) yields small, blue-black berries. Resourceful Cowgirls quickly learned to make jelly from the berries.

This recipe comes from Ardith Comstock, who says she grew up thinking Oregon grape was the only berry in the world. Even the discovery of strawberries, blackberries, and raspberries didn't sway her first love.

Wash the berries and put them in a heavy saucepan. Crush them with a potato masher. Add a little water, bring to a boil, and cook over moderate heat for 10 minutes.

Strain the juice through a jelly bag or cheesecloth (a Western-style bandana will do).

To each cup of strained juice, add 1½ cups of sugar. Mix well and bring to a boil. Boil and stir until the sugar is completely dissolved. Skim off the blue foam. Boil until thickened. Pour into hot, sterilized jelly jars.

Serve with hot biscuits. (page 7)

Makes eight 8-ounce jars of jelly

Camping Out

The Cowgirl's
First-Aid Kit

☞ A little whiskey works as a liniment for your horse's sore legs, and you can take a little for your sore anything.

☞ A shot or two of gin relieves menstrual cramps. You can also chill it and use as a compress for sprains.

☞ If you get thrown from your horse and have an abrasion, first clean the wound. Petroleum jelly applied to a clean wound has been found to act as a protective shield and speeds healing. Spider webs (usually found in a barn) also help heal the wound. Honey works wonders.

☞ Bee stings can be treated with mud. The mud draws out the sting and the stinger. Baking soda will neutralize the bee serum.

☞ Wasp bites can be soothed with vinegar.

☞ Mosquito bites will lessen with a dab of household ammonia. To avoid the bites in the first place, use baby oil as a repellent—mosquitoes don't like to put their feet in it! Did you know that one garlic capsule (or three cloves of garlic) a day will repel mosquitoes? (It also repels everything and everyone else, but you will be bite free!) The old-time Cowgirls say that bear grease is the best remedy for keeping "skeeters" off, but it's hard to get ahold of these days.

☞ Bruises should be treated with a cold compress first, and then witch hazel or slices of raw potato.

☞ If you forget to wear your hat and get a sunburn, aloe vera gel is soothing. Tea works well, too—steep two or three tea bags in one cup of water and apply with cotton pads. Or, soak in a lukewarm bath to which baking soda or oatmeal has been added.

☞ New cowboy boots can cause blisters. A time-honored way of avoiding this is to fill the new boots with boiling water, pour out the water, and then put the boots on with the socks you intend to wear with them. Let the boots dry on your feet. They will conform beautifully to your own personal bunions.

☞ Always wear gloves on your hands when working around or with horses or cattle.

☞ Cuts should be treated with comfrey. Moisten the dry herb with water or bruise the fresh leaves and lay them over the wound.

☞ Carry a penny in your pocket. Place it on a bee or wasp sting, and the wound won't hurt, swell, or itch.

Real Cowgirl's Granola

1 cup canola oil
3/4 cup honey or pure maple syrup
1 teaspoon vanilla
1 teaspoon salt
6 cups quick oats
2 cups wheat germ
1/2 cup whole wheat flour
1 cup dry milk
2 cups raw nuts, such as almonds, walnuts, pecans, or peanuts

Combine oil, honey or syrup, vanilla, and salt in a small saucepan over low heat until warm.

In a medium bowl, combine oats, wheat germ, flour, dry milk, and nuts. Stir the liquid and pour over the dry ingredients. Mix well. At this point you can use your imagination and add raisins, dried fruits cut into small pieces, and/or sunflower or sesame seeds.

Preheat oven to 250 degrees. Put the granola in a buttered 9x15-inch oblong pan and bake for about 1 1/2 hours. Watch that it does not get too brown.

Allow granola to cool. Cut into squares and store in an airtight container or plastic bags.

In her book, *There's a Mule Under My Saddle*, Jean Brown has this granola for you to pack into your saddlebags for energy. It's hearty and full of flavor and texture!

Makes 15 bars

Campfire Coffee

An old coffee pot, preferably graniteware
2 heaping tablespoons ground coffee per person
1 tablespoon salt
Fresh and cold water
1 eggshell, broken into medium-size pieces

Joie Smith lives high up on the flanks of Mount Hood in a log cabin. Joie loves nothing more than camping with her horses and her friends. Three meals a day cooked over a roaring campfire is part of the magic. The rest of the time is spent riding the trails. You become instantly awake on cold mountain mornings with Joie's coffee, done in a battered old graniteware pot, blackened by many fires. "Always bury the grounds under a tree," Joie advises.

Pour the water into the coffee pot, filling nearly to the brim. Put the pot over the fire and add the coffee. Add the salt.

When the coffee starts to boil, remove the pot from the fire and put the eggshell pieces in. The shells will cause the coffee grounds to settle to the bottom.

Keep the coffee warm beside the fire, but don't allow it to boil again.

Bury the grounds under a tree later.

"I've been around, believe me, and nothing compares to the great outdoors."

—JANE WESTLUND, Forest Service Packer, 1928–1935

Campfire Dutch Chicken

A Dutch oven with a good, tight-fitting lid

A hot fire in a pit with coals

1 chicken, cut into serving pieces

4 carrots, peeled and diced

4 potatoes, peeled and diced

2 onions, peeled and diced

Salt and pepper to taste

1 (16-ounce) can whole tomatoes, including the juice

1/2 cup cooking oil

Start the fire 1 hour before cooking. When it has burned down a little, rake out some coals. Be sure to keep the remaining coals hot.

Put a little oil in the bottom of the Dutch oven and add the chicken. Fry it over the coal fire until golden. Then add the vegetables, seasonings, and tomatoes with juice. Stir it all up and put the lid on the Dutch oven.

Put the Dutch oven directly into the pit and shovel the coals back on top of the lid. Then shovel dirt onto the hot coals. You have "sealed the oven."

One and a half hours later, carefully dig the Dutch oven out. Remove the lid, let the chicken and vegetables cool down a little, and enjoy a real campfire dinner.

Serves 6

In September 1995, Joan Triplett, Joanna Stewart, and I hit the road and traveled east from Portland up the Columbia River Gorge, headed to the Pendleton Round-Up, and then went on to the Eagle Cap Wilderness in the Wallowa Mountains for a pack trip.

Our packer and guide, Charlie, along with his wife and son, provided the mules, horses, and wonderful food. We rode all day up the Lostine River. We headed for the Eagle Cap, where we made camp that night at 6,000 feet, right at the base of the granite peak and on the shore of the pristine and icy waters of a tiny Alpine lake.

Charlie soon had a fire pit dug and a roaring fire going, while his wife attended to the other chores to feed three very hungry Cowgirls. When Charlie was getting the Dutch oven ready to put into the pit, the lid slipped and some of the hot coals fell into the chicken/vegetable mix. He smiled sheepishly and said, "Don't tell my wife. I think it will be fine."

We kept the secret, and it was fine. Just an occasional "crunch" now and then.

This is what we ate that beautiful night, with a full moon coming up. The mules and horses were hobbled, and we could hear them grazing the Alpine meadow while we devoured the entire dish.

How to Make a Cardboard Oven

1 strong, undamaged, corrugated cardboard box (The best ones
   can be obtained at your wine and liquor store.)
1 roll silver duct tape
1 large roll 25-inch, heavy-duty aluminum foil
2 disposable aluminum cake pans or pie plates that will fit
   in the bottom of your box
A sharp knife or box cutter
3–4 heavy-gauge wire coat hangers
Wire cutters
Pliers
1 nail
Pencil
Measuring tape
A pair of scissors
1 small (4.5 lb.) bag charcoal briquettes for your heat source

1. To seal the box, use the duct tape to close over all the holes
   from the outside of the box from which heat could escape when
   the oven is in use. You will have to close and seal the top of the
   box, too. (A hot-glue gun works well.) To cut the door, orient
   the box so that it is sitting on end and the longer sides of the
   box are running up and down (vertically). Using your knife,
   cut a door in the front of the box so that the whole front opens
   like a refrigerator door.

2. To line the box with foil, rotate the box so that the door is on
   top. Carefully unroll and mold the aluminum foil so that it cov-
   ers the inside of the oven from back to front and side to side,
   twice. Make sure you include the inside of the door during this
   step. Extend the foil for at least an inch on the outsides of the
   box. This is where you will duct tape the foil securely to the
   outside. Do not put tape inside the box, as it will burn during
   use. Next, make a pad of foil at least 4–6 layers thick that will
   fit over the interior bottom of the box.

My thanks to Mary
Huntington for this
amazing way to enjoy
hot cookies, muffins, and
anything else your heart
desires out on the trail!

A cardboard oven is
easy to make and use. It
can bake anything you
would try in your own
oven at home and makes
baking an additional
option when developing
camping menus.

3. To put in the oven racks, use a pencil and measuring tape to draw a horizontal line on the sides of the box on either side of the door. This line should be ⅔ of the way up the box from the bottom. Along this line, evenly mark 3 or 4 holes, depending on how many wires you are putting through the box for resting baking pans. Carefully pierce the cardboard with the nail. Cut open the wire hangers and straighten. Push each hanger wire through the marked holes. Bend the lead end at a right angle, then, while gently pulling on the wire to make tension, cut the other end of the wire to the correct length so that when the second end is bent, the wire is held tight between the box walls. Repeat this step until all the wires are in place.

4. To put in the briquette pans, take one of the foil cake pans and put it upside-down in the bottom of the oven. Put the second foil cake pan on top of the first, right-side up. For extra protection for the bottom of the box, put some sand or vermiculite in the top pan.

5. Heat is controlled by the addition of briquettes. One briquette equals 40 degrees of heat. For example, 360 degrees would be obtained with 9 briquettes. Light more briquettes than you will need and add extras as needed, especially if you are baking for a long period of time (longer than 30 minutes). Use tongs to add the briquettes to the oven, put the item to be baked on the rack, then close the door securely during baking time.

The oven is safe to place on a table, as the bottom doesn't get very warm. For extra safety, place two bricks or pieces of wood under the oven while in use to protect the surface it sits on. Do not allow children to open the oven or play around it while it is in use.

Enjoy your outdoor baked creations!

Kathy's Orange-Cranberry Cake

Out in the woods you have to be prepared. This recipe is for use in the cardboard oven, and, as you can see, this Cowgirl knows how to prepare beforehand for wonderful results! Not out in the woods? Then make these in your oven at home.

At home

1 orange, cut into sections
1/2 cup orange juice
1 egg
1/4 cup vegetable oil
1 teaspoon baking powder
1 1/2 cups flour
3/4 cup sugar
1 teaspoon baking soda
1 teaspoon salt
1/2 cup dried cranberries

Preheat oven to 350 degrees. Put the orange, juice, egg, and oil into a food processor and blend together until smooth.

In a large bowl, combine the flour, sugar, baking soda, and salt. Pour the liquid over the dry ingredients and gently mix together. Add the cranberries.

Pour batter into a greased 8x8-inch pan. Bake for 15 minutes.

Serves 8

How to Make Kathy's Cake
While Camping Out

Here is where you can get creative and fun! When you are planning a menu for horse camping, bring along the ingredients to make Kathy's Orange-Cranberry Cake! You'll just need to make a few adjustments for outdoor cooking.

Take a small can of frozen orange juice concentrate and store it in a cool spot in your pack boxes. Where the recipe calls for the cut-up orange and orange juice, blend about 1¹/₂ cups warm water with enough frozen orange juice concentrate to make a thick blend of orange juice.

Pack the dried, grated peel of an orange and add it to the dry ingredients. You can substitute powdered whole egg for the egg if you can find a source—usually a health food store.

As for the oil, I have tried blending the oil into the dry ingredients and bringing this mixture in a ziplock bag, or I have just added oil as called for in the recipe. Either way gives satisfactory results.

The dried cranberries will absorb a lot of the fluid from the muffins unless you rehydrate them in some warm water for about 15 minutes. In your pack box, keep the ingredients for the muffins in a labeled, large zipped-tight bag along with the recipe and an 8x8-inch disposable, or aluminum cake pan.

When you are ready to make the cake, prepare the wet ingredients and stir them into the dry ingredients along with the rehydrated cranberries. Have the box oven preheated with 9 or 10 hot briquettes, with a few to spare on the side. Fill the cake pan with the mix, place the pan on the rack, close the oven tightly, and bake for about 15 minutes.

Cut the cake into 9 large squares and enjoy them hot! Serve with slices of cheese and fresh fruit.

Index

Credits

clipart.com: pp. iii, ix, 6, 9, 10 (border), 12, 13 (photo), 14, 15, 16, 18, 22, 23, 19, 20, 22, 23, 30, 34, 35, 36, 38, 39, 40, 43, 46, 50, 53, 59, 60, 63, 64, 71, 72, 74, 76, 83, 84, 88

p. v. Three Cowgirls in the Three Sisters. From left to right: Joan Triplett, Joanna Stewart, and Jill Stanford. From the author's collection.

Shutterstock.com: pp. vi, vii, xi, 7, 11, 13 (background), 29, 31, 41, 47, 51, 57, 58, 67, 80, 92

p. xii, Miss Mary Robinson of Walla Walla, Washington, Queen of the 1936 Pendleton Roundup. From the author's collection.

p. 1, Cowgirls. Courtesy of the Denver Public Library, Western History Collection, Ralph Doubleday photographer, #Z-641.

p. 2, Photo by Jill Stanford.

p. 5, Pendleton Cowgirl Company #12729348. Used with permission.

p. 8. Miss Annie Oakley, "Little Sure Shot". Courtesy of the Denver Public Library, Western History Collection, Elliot & Fry, #Z-330.

p. 10, "Double Duty" © 1987 Barbara Van Cleve, used with permission.

p. 21. Women branding a calf on the Becker Ranch in the San Luis Valley, Colorado, 1884. Courtesy Colorado Historical Society, #F5441/10025494. All rights reserved.

p. 24. Mrs. Jack Elliot, Jr., ca. 1900. Courtesy Denver Public Library, Western History Collection, Rocky Mtn. Photo, #Z-626

p. 26. Photo by Harry H. Buckwalter of a woman holding a rope and wearing a holstered gun, 1905. Courtesy Colorado Historical Society #851/20031 1278. All Rights Reserved.

p. 33, John, Jean, June, and Darrell Leavitt prepare for a day of branding. Lakeview, Oregon, about 1961. Courtesy of June Leavitt.

p. 37. Feeding the chickens, 1900. Courtesy Colorado Historical Society, #CHS L256/200000 256.

p. 42, Rodeo Cowgirls. Pendleton Cowgirl Company #12729530. Used with permission.

p. 45, Sharie Ford takes care of Tallulah and Riley at a team-penning. Photo by Jill Stanford

p. 49, "With Best Wishes from Jane." Denver Public Library, Western History Collection, Z-642.

p. 52, Oregon Pinto Breeder Association 1986 Queen and Court, winner of the Rose Festival Parade. From the author's collection.

p. 54. A western Colorado horsewoman, circa 1900. Courtesy Colorado Historical Society, CHS X-6970/200006 970.

p. 55. ZA Ranch Kitchen. Courtesy Colorado Historical Society #F7634/10031 199. All rights reserved.

p. 62. "Champion of All" Kitty Canutt. Pendleton Cowgirl Company #12729349. Used with permission.

p. 65. Donna Gill. From the author's collection.

p. 68. Cowgirl and stunt girl Liz Dixon. Photo courtesy Elizabeth Dixon.

p. 73. "Spinning the Wedding Ring." Pendleton Cowgirl Company, #12729413. Used with permission.

p. 77. Horse show. Denver Public Library, Western History Collection, #Z-7261.

p. 79. Barrel racing, possibly in Sterling, Colorado. Denver Public Library, Western History Collection, #Z-624.

p. 81, Rose Smith on Jiggs. Denver Public Library, Western History Collection, #Z-638.

p. 82. Portrait of a real cowgirl, Bertha Kaepernick. Courtesy of Joanna Stewart.

p. 85, Model Camp Kitchen. Denver Public Library, Western History Collection, Z-1993.

p. 86, The start of a pack trip. Denver Public Library, Western History Collection, M.S. Wolle, Photographer #X5244

p. 89, Pack animals await further instructions. Photo by Jill Stanford.

p. 91, Homemade cardboard oven. Photo courtesy of Mary Huntington.

p. 97, The author on Indian. Photo by Chuck "The Kid" Warren.

Author Notes and Resources

- For more information on the book *Lamb Country Cooking*, by Jill Stanford, write to:

  > Countryside Publications, Ltd.
  > W11564 State Highway 64
  > Withee, WI 54498

- To hear more old-time western songs such as "I Want To Be a Real Cowboy Girl," sung by the Girls of the Golden West, write to:

  > New World Records
  > 75 Broad St. #2400
  > New York, NY 10004

  Or go online to Amazon.com and type in "Back in the Saddle"— New World Records.

- To obtain more information about Barbara Van Cleve (www .barbaravancleve.com) and her images of western women, write to:

  > Museum of New Mexico Press
  > P.O. Box 2087
  > Santa Fe, NM 87504

- There is nothing in the world like camping out and cooking and eating under the stars and wide western skies. I highly recommend the book *There's a Mule Under My Saddle Cookbook* by Jean Brown (Clinton Jones, CHJ Publishing, 1103 West Main, Middleton, Idaho 83644, ISBN 0-927022-65-6, copyright 2002). This is the "bible" for going out into the backcountry for a day, a week, or longer. Everything you need to know is in the book, from a pack trip checklist to wonderful recipes.

- To obtain Pendleton Cowgirl Company cards and more must-have cowgirl stuff, go to www.cowgirlcafeonline.com

About the Author

JILL CHARLOTTE STANFORD lives and writes in Sisters, Oregon. Visit her at www.jillcharlotte.com.